First Facts™

Science Tools

Balances

by Adele Richardson

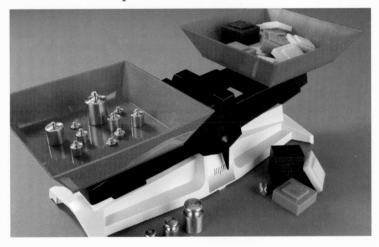

Consultant:
Dr. Ronald Browne
Associate Professor of Elementary Education
Minnesota State University, Mankato

Capstone
press

Mankato, Minnesota

First Facts is published by Capstone Press
151 Good Counsel Drive, P.O. Box 669, Mankato, Minnesota 56002
www.capstonepress.com

Library of Congress Cataloging-in-Publication Data
Richardson, Adele, 1966–
     Balances / by Adele Richardson.
     p. cm.—(First facts. Science tools)
     Summary: Introduces the function, parts, and uses of balances, and provides
instructions for two activities that demonstrate how a balance works.
     Includes bibliographical references and index.
     ISBN 0-7368-2516-9 (hardcover)
     1. Balances (Weighing instruments)—Juvenile literature. [1. Balances (Weighing
instruments)] I. Title. II. Series.
QC107.R53 2004
681'.2—dc22   2003013362

Editorial Credits
Christopher Harbo, editor; Juliette Peters, designer; Deirdre Barton, photo researcher;
     Eric Kudalis, product planning editor

Photo Credits
Capstone Press/Gary Sundermeyer, 1, 4, 5, 6, 7, 9, 10, 11, 12, 13, 16, 17, 18
Capstone Press/GEM Photo Studio/Dan Delaney, cover
Corbis/Bettmann, 20; Roger Ressmeyer, 14
Photo Researchers Inc./Science Photo Library/David Leah, 15

1 2 3 4 5 6 09 08 07 06 05 04

Table of Contents

The Class Investigates

Mrs. Gibson's class wants to know if a tennis ball weighs more than an orange. A ball and an orange are close to the same size. But they have different **weights**.

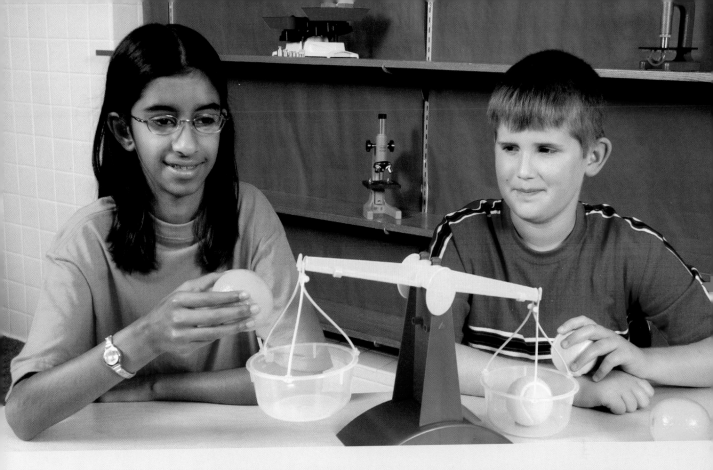

The students use a balance to find out which object weighs more. They put a tennis ball in one of the balance's cups. They put an orange in the other cup.

Turn to page 19 to try this activity!

What Is a Balance?

A balance is a type of scale. It compares the weights of different objects. The side of a balance that is lower holds the heavier object.

If a balance stays **level**, the objects weigh the same. The marbles on this balance weigh the same as the ice.

Parts of a Balance

This equal-arm balance has cups, a **beam**, and a **fulcrum**. The two cups hold objects. The cups sit on the ends of the beam. A fulcrum is under the beam. It holds up the beam.

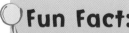

Fun Fact:
A seesaw on a playground is a type of balance.

cups

beam

fulcrum

9

Ounces and Grams

People use weights with a balance. Weights help people find out how much an object weighs. Most weights are made in **ounces** or **grams**.

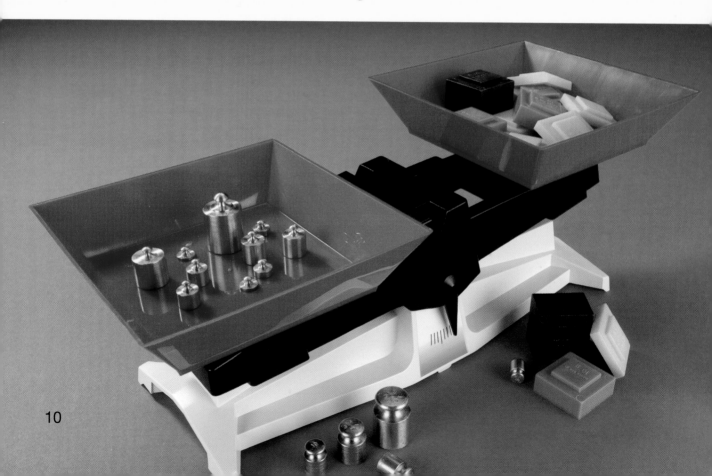

Ounces are often used in the United States. Other countries use grams. This girl adds gram weights to the balance to see how much the rocks weigh.

Balances in School

Students use balances to learn about mass. Mass is a measure of the amount of **matter** in an object. This class is testing the mass of things with similar sizes.

The class compares the mass of a clay ball and a Ping-Pong ball. The clay weighs more. It has a greater mass than the Ping-Pong ball.

Other Uses for Balances

Scientists use balances. This scientist uses a balance to weigh **aerogel** and two candies. The aerogel looks larger, but it weighs the same as the two candies.

 Fun Fact:
Aerogel is a superlight material. Aerogel was used on the *Stardust* spacecraft. Aerogel collects tiny pieces of dust from comets.

Scientists also use electronic balances. These balances do not compare the weight of two objects. Electronic balances measure the exact weight of one object.

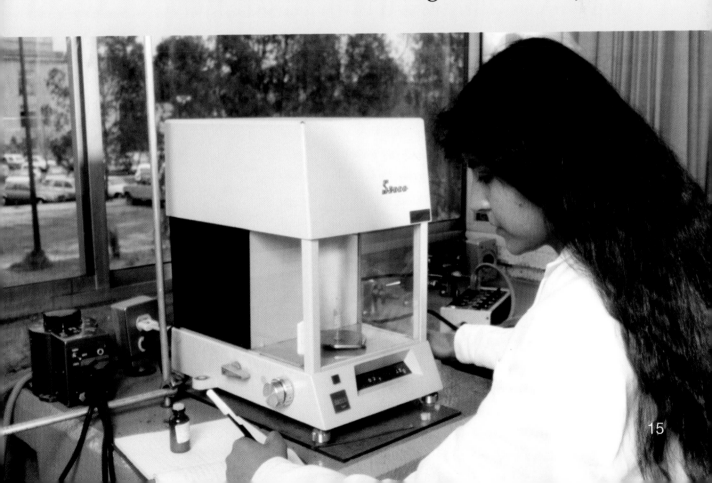

A balance is easy to make. You can build one with materials found in your classroom or your house. See how many objects you can weigh with your balance.

Try It!

What You Need

2 small paper cups
tape
12-inch (30-centimeter)
    ruler
large crayon
modeling clay
various coins
small paper clips

What You Do

1. Tape one paper cup to each end of the ruler.
2. Lay the crayon on a flat surface.
3. Stick a small piece of modeling clay on each side of the crayon. The clay keeps the crayon from rolling.
4. Place the ruler on top of the crayon. The 6-inch (15-centimeter) mark should be right on top of the crayon.
5. Place a coin in one cup. Add paper clips one at a time to the other cup. Count the paper clips used when the cups balance.

What Did They Learn?

Mrs. Gibson's class wanted to find out which weighed more, a tennis ball or an orange. Which one do you think weighs more? Let's find out.

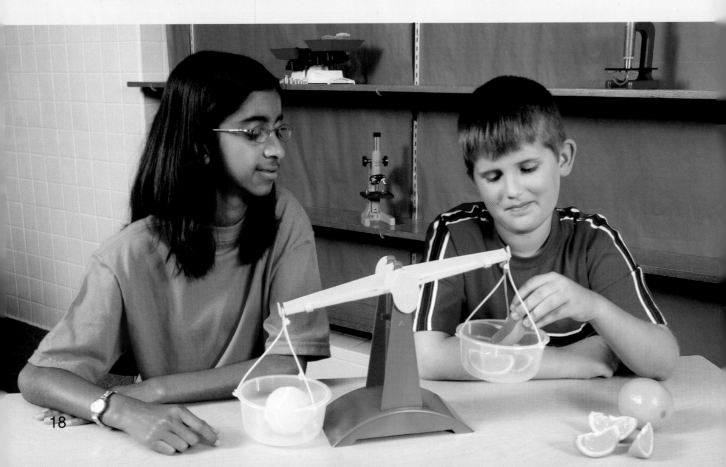

Try It!

What You Need

equal-arm balance   adult helper
tennis ball   knife
orange

What You Do

Part 1
1. Place the balance on a flat surface.
2. Set the tennis ball in one cup.
3. Place the orange in the other cup.

Which is heavier, the orange or the tennis ball? What is inside the orange? What do you think is inside a tennis ball?

Part 2
1. Take the orange off the balance.
2. Ask an adult to cut the orange into six or eight wedges.
3. Add the orange back to the cup one wedge at a time. Stop when the orange wedges and the tennis ball balance. If necessary, cut an orange wedge in half to level the balance.

How many orange slices did it take to equal the weight of the tennis ball?

Amazing But True!

Balances have not always been used for science. Fur traders once used steelyard balances. These balances had a beam with a long arm and a short arm. The short arm held furs. The long arm held a weight. The weight slid up and down the arm to find the balancing point. Trappers were paid by the weight of the furs they trapped.

What Do You Think?

1. A balance is a scale. People use scales to weigh many things. Where are scales used? What kinds of objects do they weigh?

2. The fulcrum of an equal-arm balance must sit under the exact center of the beam. What would happen if the fulcrum were not in the center?

3. A glass of water has more mass than an empty glass. Which one would weigh more? How could you be sure?

4. When two objects on a balance stay level, what do you know about their weights?

Glossary

aerogel (AIR-uh-jel)—a superlight material that is 99 percent air

beam (BEEM)—a straight piece of plastic or metal that holds the cups or pans of a balance

fulcrum (FUL-krum)—the point on which the beam of a balance rests

gram (GRAHM)—a metric unit of measurement equal to one-thousandth of a kilogram

level (LEV-uhl)—even on both sides

matter (MAT-ur)—anything that has weight and takes up space

ounce (OUNSS)—an inch-pound unit of measurement equal to one-sixteenth of a pound

weight (WATE)—a measurement of how heavy something is, or an object used to measure how heavy something is

Read More

Bullock, Linda. *You Can Use a Balance.* Rookie Read-About Science. New York: Children's Press, 2003.

Pallotta, Jerry. *Hershey's Milk Chocolate Weights and Measures.* New York: Scholastic/Cartwheel Books, 2002.

Internet Sites

FactHound offers a safe, fun way to find Internet sites related to this book. All of the sites on FactHound have been researched by our staff.

Here's how:
1. Visit *www.facthound.com*
2. Type in this special code **0736825169** for age-appropriate sites. Or enter a search word related to this book for a more general search.
3. Click on the Fetch It button.

FactHound will fetch the best sites for you!

Index